Previous Books

Stubby Pencil Poems of Rural Livin' Doin's
Stubby Pencil Poems of Great Basin Musin's

Stubby Pencil Poems
of
High Desert Viewin's

G. B. GRIFFITH

BALBOA.PRESS

A DIVISION OF HAY HOUSE

Balboa Press books may be ordered through booksellers or by contacting:

Balboa Press
A Division of Hay House
1663 Liberty Drive
Bloomington, IN 47403
www.balboapress.com
1 (877) 407-4847

Because of the dynamic nature of the Internet, any web addresses or links contained in this book may have changed since publication and may no longer be valid. The views expressed in this work are solely those of the author and do not necessarily reflect the views of the publisher, and the publisher hereby disclaims any responsibility for them.

The author of this book does not dispense medical advice or prescribe the use of any technique as a form of treatment for physical, emotional, or medical problems without the advice of a physician, either directly or indirectly. The intent of the author is only to offer information of a general nature to help you in your quest for emotional and spiritual well-being. In the event you use any of the information in this book for yourself, which is your constitutional right, the author and the publisher assume no responsibility for your actions.

Any people depicted in stock imagery provided by Getty Images are models, and such images are being used for illustrative purposes only. Certain stock imagery © Getty Images.

Print information available on the last page.

ISBN: 978-1-9822-4079-0 (sc)
ISBN: 978-1-9822-4080-6 (e)

Balboa Press rev. date: 01/02/2020

Dedication

To Kate, Misty, Shiloh and Sadie. Miss you all.

Contents

Poetry Magic

An introduction

These are short and some ain't exactly neat.

A moment for you to pause and wonder some.
With meanings you'll find discrete.
But through the magic of poetry, you'll see the answers come.

High Desert Viewin'

The Bitterbrush are all a poppin'.

Their blossoms of yellow-gold.
Baby Cottontails are busy a hoppin'.
Ready to leave their mama's fold.

Spring is a bustin' out all over enhancing my high desert viewin'.
Of the native brush and critters each a offerin' their own special prize.
Crediting Mother Nature to her unique ways a doin'.
For bringing pleasure to these winter sore eyes.

Pencil Poetry

A calling, this need to write.

Putting my brain in gear, prompting me to think.
Each work a puzzle to make it all fit right.
Getting a boost from having some wine to drink.

Not writing for fame or wage.
Telling these stories; oh what fun.
It's a struggle at times, translating thought to page.
Asking for divine intervention to get 'em done.

Being grateful for where all the words come from.
Along with the pleasure of attaching verb to noun.
Taking liberty with the English language some.
Grateful for my pencil in catching up and writing 'em all
down.

Relationships

Ever wonder what our horses think of us.

Of our strange ways and all the things we tend to do.
That makes them happy or brings them to cuss.
Assuming they know those kinds of words too.

Under saddle, submitting to our will.
Regarding us as pard'ners in that special way they do.
But when they are moody, we're guaranteed a spill.
Changing up their minds, we do it too.

Sometimes they like us, sometimes they don't.
Depends on us and what we're wanting them to do.
Sometimes they will, sometimes they won't.
They can have good days or bad days too.

Sizin' 'em Up

One size doesn't fit 'em all.

Some are big. Some are small.
There's in-betweeners, my studyin' and measurin' 'em with my eyes where they fall.
Those green, elongated shaped balls, the result of my horses' nature call.

Assuming the bigger the horse, the bigger the "doo".
My research finding that it's seldom true.
Perhaps the secret is in the processing as the grass and alfalfa passes through.
The horses watching me wondering, why is this so important to you?

My Leaky Bucket

Me and my leaky bucket with water to haul.

Cussing that bucket for the water it lost.
Some fifty feet from the faucet to each horses' stall.
Angry at myself for the time that it cost.

My leaky bucket, drip upon drip.
My face a'frowning from watching the water fall.
Marking our trail, trip after trip.
There'd a been more if there'd been no bucket at all.

Lonely Vigil

The gelding stood next to the down mare.

In his lonely vigil, he seemed to know.
Watching over her body where,
her time had come and she had to go.

It was not his choice that she left.
For hours he stood beside her all alone.
Her death left him bereft;
She was gone, his sorrow shown.

Screaming his displeasure when the other horses came.
Stay away – she was my friend.
Without her there, his life would never be the same.
Declaring his devotion to her at her end.

Bidding his final farewell.
His grief for her fully expressed.
Left that place where she fell.
Let her be. Let her rest.

Wash Me

In town for a load of feed.

And stopping by the hardware store.
Picking up all the things we need.
Seeing "Wash Me" scrawled across my pick-up's door.

Those words written in that dried up muck.
From the dust and mud, we travel through.
There's no shame – it's a working truck.
If only that person who wrote those words only knew.

The box of staples was for mending a fence.
The bed was full of bales of hay.
Besides, the dirt hid all of its scratches and dents.
That washing the truck meant for a wasted day.

Sagebrush Campfire

Cussing because their eyes stung from the acrid smoke.

That sank into their clothing and followed 'em wherever they sat.
Voices had to be cleared before they spoke.
The words caught in their throats, released only after they coughed and spat.

Long stories of the range and cowboying told and shared since last they met.
No one wanting to talk was ignored or spurned,
with faces silhouetted from the glow of a non-filtered cigarette.
All of 'em knowing their place at that campfire was fairly earned.

Hearty laughter at embellished tales they knew just couldn't be true.
And listened intently to those who spoke from their heart.
Sagebrush branches burned 'til all the stories were done and tales were through.
Ended with a vow to gather again and a 'best a luck' to each other as they part.

Song Dogs

Bawl mouthed dogs when on the run.

Sing in delight their hunting song.
Their blue tinged coats shown off by the sun.
In finding scent, they're seldom ever wrong.

Baying in octaves when they sound.
Theirs' is a yodeled tune finely played.
The meaning known only to the Bluetick Hound.
In as a sweet a voice that was ever made.

Grammar "Slips"

Please excuse us for our saying don't.

Instead of doesn't – that seems too slow.
For saying yes or no, we simply won't.
Preferring our yeps and nopes and it just ain't so.

There's time when we've cussed.
Letting 'em slip but only when the time is right.
Know it all comes from our grammar rust.
So, you'll understand when our English ain't all that tight.

We shove words together that weren't meant to be.
Our got'ta from got to, we learned in our teens.
When it comes to verbs of bein', there's no use for the g.
And got no, well, we know what that means.

So when you hear we us use 'em and let a double negative go.
Our English is fine with us, please be assured.
It don't need no fixin', it just ain't so.
Just like us, it got no need to be cured.

The Chosen Few

Wearing plaid cotton shirts and flat-heeled boots,

denim jeans and a sweat stained hat.
Having no use for three-piece suits,
polished shoes or any other things quite like that.

A life spent outside, breathing clean fresh air.
Preferring it to the sights and sounds of town.
Taking pleasure from being out there.
Waking with the sun, resting only after it went down.

Sweating due to the summer heat.
In winter, there were times we froze.
Working hard 'till we were beat.
It's the life we love, the life we chose.

Or perhaps we never really had a say.
We were chosen before we even knew.
From the many to be made this way.
To be one of the lucky few.

These Hard Men

These hard men of yore.

Whose tools; their horse, a saddle and a rawhide rope.
Chasing another man's herd for a dollar a day, seldom more.
A hard life lived on a near empty belly but a heart full of hope.

There's no doubting their pride.
Owning little more than what they rode and the cloths they wore.
Their purpose was to drive and ride.
Ending each long day tired and sore.

Barely older than boys, giving them that name.
The west was their place for what they saw in the promise there
Becoming legends, gaining them their fame.
Too few of 'em lived 'till old age to tell their stories from their rocking chair.

G. B. Griffith

Under That Sage

Together they laid.

Two young jack rabbits from fear of a winter storm's rage.
Seeking shelter, they stayed,
under that sage.

The snow fell and piled high.
Entrapping them in nature's unintended cage.
They never knew their time was nigh,
under that sage.

Wan'na, Gon'na, Got'ta

I am a gon'na.

Put a halter on ya.
Run away, all ya wan'na.
I'll chase ya, then I'll a catch ya.

Throw a tantrum, if ya got'ta.
Throw your head, if ya wan'na.
Shy away, if ya gon'na.
I'm a staying, 'till I got ya.

I am gon'na ride ya.
Ya don't wan'na, now don't ya.
Just to let ya know, throwing me is a gon'na haunt ya.
Don't forget, who comes out to feed ya.

Joe

Thick and black, my cup of Joe.

No cream or sugar, just like those from my service days.
It prompts me to move and gets my blood to flow.
And jolts my mind awake from its pre-dawn haze.

My aching hands are wrapped tight around that coffee cup.
Full of that steaming hot, soothing brew.
It's proven over again its worth in fixing me up.
From all those years of working outside, 'till my work was
through.

For now, the chores and feeding are done.
Though I can't help wondering; what would horses do if
given some Joe.
To help them with the cold and their aches while waiting
for the warming sun.
In that they're horses, I'll probably never know.

Horse, Dog, Man

Hackamore, its headstall, and saddle are put away.
Against the barn wall loaded alongside all the tack.
They've been brushed off, ready for another day.
One on its hook, the other on its rack.

Couldn't have figured on or hoped for a better day.
Horse, dog and man out together for a pleasure ride.
Only God and nature witnessed the harmony of it all; my
wondering what they'd say.
Horse and man as one, the dog never ventured far from
our side.

Some sweet alfalfa as a treat after smoothing away my
horse's sweat.
Her head and neck level with her shoulders, standing in
the sun for a nap.
My feet are up, a beer be'd good, but I won't get up quite yet.
The dog is asleep on the couch beside me, his head on
my lap.

Favorite Jeans

They've got holes with both knees torn.

They're not too loose and not too tight.
Faded plenty from being worn.
With a tug of the belt they fit just right.

For all their rips and tears, I'm to blame.
From barbed wire tussles, every battle lost.
To hay hook misses, from my faulty aim.
A pocket torn when my mare got spunky and I got tossed.

Pard'ners, I consider them to be.
Though they may be wearin' a bit too thin.
I'll stick with them and they with me.
I finally got 'em to where they're nearly broken in.

Eye to Eye

Standing. Looking. Eye to eye.

My old bay mare and I.
Studying each other, knowing why.
On our good days, now gone by.

She always accepted saddle and tack.
My words of thanks are accompanied with a heavy sigh.
For the privilege of her allowing me on her back.
Best said to her, eye to eye.

G. B. Griffith

Driving with Dogs

My dogs helping me drive my truck.

Sitting right beside me next to my hip.
The road is bumpy, I'm cursing our luck.
Slobber swinging from both of their lip(s).

They're not concerned by any driving rule.
Or roadside signs aiming to limit our speed.
They're shaking their heads, slinging their drool.
Last I heard, dogs can't read.

Windshield's covered with their dried nose smears.
From watching for rabbit in case they show.
The dogs go crazy while I'm shifting gears.
Knocking it into neutral; the truck can't go.

A rabbit running, hey driver can't you see.
Get it in gear and push it to the metal.
Bad for them but good for me;
their legs can't reach the pedal.

Release the Hens

Tens of thousands, to say the least.

Mormon Crickets, hopping along, moving abreast.
Every one of them fat and juicy from their desert feast.
Searching for more in their never-ending feeding quest.

Chickens in their pen, wide-eyed from what they see.
Ignoring every bit of their normal feed.
A cricket, gourmet meal it could be.
If only they would be freed.

Dinner awaits them outside their gate.
Appeasing their appetite for cricket all depends
on a helping hand to end their wait,
to open the latch and release the hens.

Boss Mare

A Declaration

I am the top mare.

The first to feed and I'll hog the water trough.
If this hurts your feelings, I simply do not care.
I'll take what I want, when I want, by running you off.

It's mine, all mine, I do declare.
I am one mean, tough ole hoss.
The barn, the stalls, the feed, I feel no need to share.
That's because I am the boss.

I'll toss my head to get my message clear.
To warn you all to get out of my way.
If you try and challenge me, I'll throw you my rear.
Or my bite will quickly bring you to bay.

Pinning my ears back usually does the trick.
To show my displeasure when my orders aren't met.
I've got most of you well in-line due to my well-aimed kick.
Except for that mule-headed gelding. He ain't learned
nothing yet.

Alfalfa and Grits

I may be an older horse but I've not lost me my wits.

Standing here a waitin' for my dinner to eat.
I do like me my alfalfa but I do love me my grits.
Those supplements you feed me, they're so tasty and sweet.

The oats, the grains are what I'm all crazy about.
Feeding me without 'em sends me to fits.
I'll toss my alfalfa, stomp my feet, then pout.
So never, don't you even, forget . . . . that I do love me my grits.

Bang Bang

Bang Bang on the corral gate.

Bang Bang it's been hours since I last ate.
Bang Bang my dinner's late.
Bang Bang don't make me wait.

My hooves as hammers, they work great.
To make my point, they fit the need.
I was hoping you'd take the bait.
For you to come on over and give me my feed.

Grass and alfalfa, I knew you would.
Sorry about the gate, I made a wreck of it.
But boy or boy did it ever feel so good.
Bang Bang, that was just for the heck of it.

Directions

Those folks live down this road a' ways.

Drive on past a rusted-up cattle guard.
Then to the right you'll see some horses at graze.
It's the same place that has an old Ford tractor sitting in
the yard.

Watch out for the dry creek bed.
There's quite a dip so drive with care.
Past that, you'll see a large pole barn, painted red.
Look for a welcome sign hung on a gate and you'll know
you're there.

Don't be surprised if along your way.
You see folks wave, it ain't nothing to fear.
Wave on back, it's just our way.
This is the country, it's a bit different out here.

G. B. Griffith

I'm Feeling It Too

52

You're shivering, though your coat is thick, heavy and coarse.

This brutal cold has you chilled all the way through.
Just letting you know, with you being my horse.
Yep, I'm feeling it too.

So, let's get on back home, get warm and mend.
It's what's best for both me and you.
Just letting you know, with you being my friend.
Yep, I'm feeling it too.

Alfalfa Bits

Bits of alfalfa in the cab of my truck.

Some on the floorboard, some on the seat.
Some on the dashboard where they got stuck.
Up near the windshield right where they meet.

Hauling those bales for my horses' giddy-up go.
Left the rear slider open, it was a brutally hot day.
Into the cab they all flew guided by the wind's flow.
Landing where they wanted and intended to stay.

I guess I could vacuum, unless I forgits.
Cleaning up those bits was my intent.
But then, I got used to all those bits.
I don't mind their company and I've grown partial to their
scent.

Fading Memories

Sitting, thinking of my times past.

Reminiscing of good days and bad.
Some details are now missing, others fading fast.
Wishing I could fix what my memory once had.

Sentimental thoughts of my horses now gone.
Their coats and names, are all that I recall.
Their quirks and the games they played, when I tried to get on.
But for some reason, I simply can't remember it all.

Looking out over my place.
At the corral where they all once stood.
Feeling a smile taking over my face.
From memories coming back and hoping more would.

Of saddling them up and tightening their cinch.
But not remembering every day that I rode.
Then feeling my body go tight, my entire self flinch.
There ain't no forgetting all the times I got throw'd.

Spoiled Dogs (?)

Some say I spoil you two.

That you lead lives of leisure with nothing to do.
But I know that it's just not true.
Because I know what a day brings for you.

Rising earlier than the dawning sun.
When most dogs are still snoozing in bed.
With a full list of chores and acres upon acres you need
to run,
critters to chase and a full day's work ahead.

I start every morning early in the kitchen makin'
your breakfast to which this question begs:
How many slices of crispy bacon?
and how do you want your eggs?

Stick

Neither fiction nor a tall country tale.

This sad saga told of a chestnut mare.
That had a large stick, stuck in the end of her tail.
It was a wonder of how it even got in there.

She didn't seem to mind,
That stick and her tail being all tangled up tight.
Even though it was so close behind, her behind.
It was such a harmless stick, at least at first sight.

The other horses gathered and thought when they saw.
What a novel idea, in fact rather bold.
Her trick with that stick, held them in awe.
Then changing their minds when seeing the drama unfold.

That fateful day,
A horsefly flew onto the chestnut mare's back.
She swung her tail mightily to spook it away.
But spooked only herself when that stick gave her a painful
whack.

Telling No Lies

With a twitch of an ear.

Sometimes both to make things clear.
Showing trust or relaying fear.
In a message you cannot hear.

Windows to their mind.
Expressing their mood be it happy or sad.
The answer's there for you to find.
Watch and learn for there's lessons to be had.

Moving them forward when on alert, listening hard.
Twisting and twirling them when they have a complaint
to lodge.
Dropping them to the side when they're easy, dropping
their guard.
Pinning them straight back, there may be hooves to dodge.

Their acceptance of, or if they deny,
our friendship – that's up to us to figure out why.
Reading their ears tells us if and when it's worth a try.
No horse will ever tell us a lie.

G. B. Griffith

The Choice

My heart goes beyond aching.

When looking at my favorite mare.
Her old age is showing though her spirit is nowhere near breaking.
Her eyes still blaze clear and are now fixed on me with her, where's dinner stare.

I'm thinking of all our years together and the hours with me on her back.
Traveling through miles of sage, moving so easy, on the go.
Learning to forgive each other's faults, allowing each other slack.
Preferring her company over that of most people I've met or have come to know.

I'm feeling a winter chill closing in, putting me ill at ease.
She's one tough old horse and I know she'll get through this bitter cold night.
But our friendship guides my choice; I don't want her to suffer in this freeze.
I'll put a blanket on her and adjust the straps so that it fits her right.

G. B. Griffith

There from Here

Can't get there from here.

Thinking of the only road that takes me to town.
When it was cut by several gulley's, deep and sheer.
From a flash flood with water running angry and brown.

My only choice is to settle on in.
With plenty to do here on the place, my gloves in hand.
I feel my face break into a face wide grin.
This country living; my animals and working outside with
views of wide-open land.

It's everything I love and treat with care.
Losing any of it is something I truly fear.
Of what the town offers; there's simply nothing for me
there.
So, I'll let that road be. I 'd rather be here.

Trust

She watched me and my every move.

From where she was laying in that way horses do.
Her ears were forward, it was her way to prove.
I was invited to approach her if I wanted to.

This wasn't the first time I had tried.
With horses, never giving up on them is a must.
When I smoothed out her forelock, she never shied.
I left her knowing, I was finally awarded with her trust.

G. B. Griffith

Who's Who?

It seems like taking care of 'em never ends.

Keeping 'em happy and healthy is our main concern.
The length of our day – that depends.
On what they need; each begrudgingly waiting their turn.

We jump when they call to us.
One loud whiney is all it takes.
Going out to determine the cause of the fuss.
Finding it's for their belly's sakes.

They've got us figured out right.
Getting us to do what they want us to do.
Who says horses ain't bright?
So, here's the question; who's training who?

Life Lesson

Cigarette papers and a tobacco tin.

All that's needed when you're making a smoke.
A lick and a twist to seal that tobacco in.
A lesson taught by an old cowpoke.

There's gon'na be times along your way.
You can bet someone's gon'na let you down.
Be careful, watch your back or you'll be the one to pay.
It's the same if you live out here or there in town.

With people, you just can't tell what you're gon'na get.
So, contemplate this the next time you're all alone.
Life is much like this cigarette.
It's best if you know how to roll your own.

Accept and For

They Accept

The headstall with the bit.
The cinch with nary a fit.
The saddle for us to sit.
to go where we say to git.

For

The company that they brought.
The patience that they taught.
Their friendship to which we owe a lot.
To help us get to that place we've always sought.

G. B. Griffith

Glass of Wine

Glass of wine, so sublime.

Tastes so fine, every time.
From the box, ain't no crime.
From the bottle, best when in its prime.

Glass of wine, shades of red.
A vision of Merlot in my head.
Or a fine Shiraz in its stead.
A reward when coming in off my spread.

Glass of wine, my friend so kind.
The best, I could hope to find.
To lay my troubles, help me unwind.
To cuddle with and to ease my mind.

Glass of wine, rain or shine.
A vintage year or fresh off the vine.
It don't matter much, it's all mine.
Here's to tomorrow and that glass of wine.

Dead-Eye Suzy

Having a conversation with that horse.

The two of us together at the scene of her crime.
She showed no sign of remorse.
For what she did, it not being her very first time.

We both know who's to blame.
Your bucket is full, but it's not water I see.
You dropped a full load with near perfect aim.
Of bobbing green apples; those not grown on a tree.

We've talked about this.
You, Dead-Eye Suzy, where do I begin.
Your bucket's no target, next time miss.
But knowing you, you'll do it again.

G. B. Griffith

A Full Day

Competing with the sun to see who gets up first.

A full day is waiting with seemingly endless chores.
The lifting and hauling, feeling their back may at any time burst.
Hands hurting, fingers suffering from open sores.

There's no time for complaining, besides there's no need.
They know what a full day of work is worth.
Getting things done is the heart and soul of their rural creed.
Next to looking forward to a new day's birth.

G. B. Griffith

Alfalfa Thieves

Seems like every barn has one or two.

Bedeviled by the presence of the alfalfa thief.
Stealing from their neighbors; it don't matter who.
Leaving them with only morsels and to their empty belly grief.

Their tactics differ but the result's the same.
Snatching from the tops of feeders or through the sides of stalls, the alfalfa's gone.
A perfected style in their thieving game.
Their victims are left forlorn, wondering what the heck is going on.

Their people scolding followed with an angry finger pointed and shook.
When seeing that the thieves' stable mates didn't eat.
The perpetrators looking all innocent with their well-practiced who me look.
But betrayed by all that alfalfa scattered around their feet.

A Crew A Two

We had work to do.

Together as usual the whole day through.
That coonhound and I making a crew a two.
We'll rest later, for us, it was nothing new.

Putting in posts and fencing though my body already aches.
There was no other choice knowing there was no excuse.
This life I chose I learned long ago what it takes.
Then turned to her and let her loose.

Jackrabbits running and bounding from her giving chase.
Sounding her bay through the rabbitbrush and sage.
She was running hard to match their pace.
And doing quite well given her age.

Both worn at the end of the day but with nothing more to prove.
She looked at me with her squinty eyed stare.
Her message was clear; you need to move.
You're sitting in my favorite chair.

20 Below

I feel the snow crunch below my toes.

My boots are nearly frozen all the way through.
It's so damned cold I can't feel my nose.
It's 20 below with the thermometer holding true.

Even the sage is huddled up close.
Branches droop, draped in snow.
The wind is providing a chill in a heavy dose.
The sun ain't helping any with it hanging so low.

I'd like to be going in.
But my horses need me right now so I won't quite yet.
Being as cold out here as it's ever been.
There's ice to break and their feed to get.

Boxes

My dogs, in small wooden boxes, sitting on a shelf.

Most of whom I've known since the day of their birth.
There's a place among them. It's for myself.
When I'll be with them again, once I leave this earth.

These Things

Broken Bones

And blood on my shirt.
My life with horses, accepting all of its knowns;
Even those that have caused me hurt.

Their bucking and well-aimed kicking.
These things they sometimes do.
Intent on delivering an old-fashioned licking.
It's only their unbroken spirits busting through.

They show no remorse when I get thrown.
Leaving me sitting in the dust, bruised and sore.
When it comes to the worst hurt I've known.
Is when they grow so old, they can't do these things no more.

Day Is Done

The Country Life

Day is Done.
Quitting only with the setting sun.
Content with what got done.
Holding no regrets, not a single one.

Can't help but smile.
Out here, hard work is still in style.
Can't beat this life, not by a mile.
Finding that it's all been worth my while.

There's been plenty of sweat.
Shirt and forehead have gotten soaking wet.
But I'm not ready to give it all up yet.
When I do, let these words serve as my epithet.

Stories of Rhyme

So why do we write these old stories of rhyme.
That speak of life and living out here on the range.
Picking up pen or pencil, reminiscing in our easy time.
Our words flowing from mind to paper, working themselves
into story no matter how strange.

We write not for money, Laureate or literary prize.
Shrugging our shoulders when the critics howl for the
English we use.
Our don'ts and ain'ts; they're not worthy in their eyes.
Not understanding that our works are done in a style we
choose.

We write 'em out of devotion with an eye past today.
Knowing our old stories of rhyme are so fleeting, so we
thought them to share.
Please read 'em, hear 'em and think about 'em is what we'd
like to say.
And keep 'em for those a'comin in your loving care.

G. B. Griffith

That Horse of Mine

She was my ride.
That sweet bay mare.
On the day she had to leave my side.
I offered you this prayer.

I now place her in your care.
She was one fine old horse, the first I looked for when the
sun lit the morning sky.
Please tend to her in your place up there.
You'll take to her – you'll soon figure out why.

Whisper sweet things in her ears.
In the same way I used to do.
She doesn't take to new places easy, so it would soothe
her fears.
I can't be there yet, so now it's all up to you.

She was my favorite of all these horses here, but then, that
you knew.
She wasn't the prettiest or fastest, but her heart was true.
She was tough, I could count on her to get us through,
Any ride or situation. It's why our friendship grew.

I hope you have the time to hear my plea.
I miss that horse of mine – that's for sure.
We came as close as a man and horse could be.
She belonged to me as much as I did to her.

G. B. Griffith

The Provider

Sitting under this cottonwood tree.
Large enough for me to rest where I please.
Inspiring me to write of what I see.
Finding the words with surprising ease.

Its branches and leaves offer plenty of places for the birds
to play.
Seeking shelter from the weather and a predator's deeds.
Selecting mates – natures call they must obey.
Preparing their nests with the trees soft cotton-like seeds.

The rest float gently down to sprout a tree.
For someone new to sit under and just like me.
Discover that it's more than just a tree.
A provider of life for those yet to be.

G. B. Griffith

A Silent Prayer

My hands, rough and worn.
From my work, I regard a gift.
For this land, these horses, gladly bourn.
Enduring through these seasons, as they shift.

In all my years, there's been no change.
Out before dawn then back past dusk.
Thanking my maker for my life here on the range.
Yet asking why he made a man's life so brusque.

On that day when I finally fade.
And he strikes my name from his book.
Let me be remembered when my soul is weighed.
That I gave more than what I took.

A Cotton Shirt, Boots and Faded Jeans

Preparing for the day my body's spent.
From the things I do and the way I live.
When heaven recalls my soul that the good Lord lent.
I'll ask for this one last favor for him to give.

Save those angel's wings for those more deserving than me.
I'm only wanting outdoor scenes,
a place for all my horses, dogs and, for me,
a cotton shirt, boots and faded jeans.

Printed in the United States
By Bookmasters